THE CHRISTIAN VISION OF GOD

THE CHRISTIAN VISION OF GOD

Alister McGrath

First published in Great Britain in 2008

Society for Promoting Christian Knowledge
36 Causton Street
London SW1P 4ST

British Library Cataloguing-in-Publication Data
A catalogue record for this book is available from the British Library

ISBN 978–0–281–05596–8

1 3 5 7 9 10 8 6 4 2

Designed and typeset by Sarah Smith
Printed in China

contents

introduction

'I believe in God.' These opening words of the Christian creeds have stood at the heart of public worship and private theological reflection for centuries. Yet they have never been understood merely to mean 'I assent to the existence of God', or 'I feel able to tick God-boxes on questionnaires'. Faith goes far beyond assenting to ideas; it has to do with active trust and commitment. To believe in God, in the deeply Christian sense of that word, is to accept and embrace God, in the full knowledge that this act of trust and commitment leads to personal and social transformation. The much neglected Anglican theologian W. H. Griffith-Thomas (1861–1924) tried to express this aspect of faith when he spoke of it as beginning with 'the conviction of the mind based on adequate evidence', continuing 'in the confidence of the heart or emotions based on conviction', and being 'crowned in the consent of the will, by means of which the conviction and confidence are expressed in conduct.' Martin Luther made a similar point, in pleading for Christians to set aside the impoverished idea of faith as mere notional assent. Faith is the trusting, transforming response of the human soul to the promises of a faithful and loving God.

Luther's comment highlights the need to clarify what sort of God Christians believe in. When we declare that we believe in God, what God are we actually talking about? After all, the great Greek philosopher Aristotle spoke of the existence of a god. Yet his idea was of a strongly impersonal God – a prime unmoved mover, who could not be known by humanity, and who certainly seemed to have no interest in changing that situation. This god was distant, remote, and uninvolved in the cares and concerns of humanity. This kind of god might be a convenient explanation for some philosophical riddles, but had little or nothing to do with the experience or lives of ordinary people.

Yet both the Old and New Testaments speak of a very different kind of God. From the outset, the God of Israel and the Christian church is vividly portrayed as one who chooses to make himself known, and to enter into a relationship with his people. God is one who loves, and who makes that love known through his actions in history. The 'God of Abraham, Isaac and Jacob' was not a philosophical idea, but a living, transforming reality. In using phrases such as 'the God and Father of our Lord Jesus Christ' (1 Peter 1.3), New Testament writers sought to place clear blue water between abstract or generic ideas of divinity, and the specific God who had called and guided Israel down the ages, and had now inaugurated a new era through the coming of Christ.

Although earlier volumes in this series have touched on aspects of the Christian understanding of God, some outstanding themes remain to be explored. What does it mean to speak of a 'personal' God? Or the 'mystery' of God? And why does the Christian church insist upon speaking of the 'three persons' of the Trinity? For many theologians, the doctrine of the Trinity is the crowning glory of the Christian faith's vision of God, bringing its individual notes together in a glorious harmony. It is fitting to end this series by giving thought to these questions, once more drawing on the conceptual and imaginative riches of the Christian tradition, including its theologians and poets, and using images designed to stimulate the imagination. For in the end, the Christian faith concerns far more than understanding and knowledge; it is about being saturated with the presence and power of a loving and living God.

Alister McGrath

God as the heart's desire

1 God as the heart's desire

Many years ago, when I was beginning to think about the themes of Christian theology, I decided to read Augustine of Hippo's *Confessions*. I knew little about Augustine (354–430), other than his famous request to God to grant him chastity (but not just yet). My reason for wanting to read him was simple. Having recently moved away from atheism to Christianity, I was naturally interested in reading about others who had experienced similar conversions. A friend had mentioned that Augustine had some things to say on this matter, and suggested I might like to read his *Confessions*. He explained that it was Augustine's spiritual autobiography, written sometime around 397. I borrowed a copy from my college library, curled up comfortably in an old armchair on a cold winter's evening with a cup of steaming cocoa, and settled down to read it.

Eventually, I came to the famous section in which he wrote about his conversion experience in a garden in the Italian city of Milan. But I had become sidetracked long before then, enchanted by Augustine's language and imagery, and the fascinating ideas that he opened up to me. I found myself pausing time after time, jotting down phrases, wishing I could express myself as well as he did. The first phrase that caught my attention in this way occurred almost immediately. Augustine opened his account of his spiritual development with a short prayer, known to many but not then to me, which included these memorable lines:

> You have made us for yourself, and our heart is restless until it finds its rest in you.

They put into words something that I had begun to appreciate, but never quite managed to articulate – that God is the true goal of the human heart and mind.

It is a highly appropriate point at which to begin our reflections on the nature of the Christian God. God comes to us, not as an unknown, but as one who has created us and known us from the beginning. We are created with a homing instinct for God, which neither sin nor doubt can entirely overwhelm. We long for our heavenly homeland, even though we are exiled on earth.

'Home is where the heart is.' This traditional saying points to a fundamental truth about human nature: our need to feel that we belong somewhere, both physically and psychologically – for home is as much a psychological as a geographical notion. We become attached to people and places. Even the Prodigal Son longed to return home to his father after his disenchantment with the 'Far Country'. He knew that was where he belonged, even though he had turned his back on it. We have been created to be with God in heaven; that is our homeland. As the *Shorter Westminster Catechism* famously put it back in 1647, 'the chief end of man is to glorify God, and enjoy him for ever.'

This idea is found in Cyprian of Carthage's treatise *On mortality*. Cyprian, a bishop who suffered a martyr's death at the hands of the Roman authorities in 251, held that Christians had nothing to fear from death, whether from persecution or natural causes, in that it was a gateway to meeting God in heaven, and returning home. In this remarkable early Christian writing, we find Cyprian anticipating reunion with the saints in glory as a means of bringing stability to his personal spiritual situation.

We regard paradise as our homeland. We have already begun to consider the patriarchs as our parents. Why do we not hasten and run, so that we may catch sight of our native land, and greet our parents? There a great number of our dear ones is awaiting us, and a dense crowd of parents, brothers, children, is longing for us, already assured

of their own safety, and still anxious for our salvation. To attain to their presence and their embrace – what a joy, both for them and for us!

The theme of God as the culmination and fulfilment of all human desire has been explored throughout Christian history. This is not to say that God is an invention, somehow conjured up by needy, inadequate people to meet their illusory desires. Nor is it to say that we mould our idea of God after the likeness of our longings. Rather, we begin from the secure theological premise that God has created us in order to relate to us, and endowed us with faculties that will enable us to find our way home, even if we need a lot of help along the way. The world has so much to offer us. Yet while such things may well be good images of what we really desire, they are no substitute for it. God, and God alone, is the one who can meet our deepest needs. God eclipses, overwhelms and overshadows even the best that this world has to offer.

This point is made with precision and power in one of the shortest gospel parables of the kingdom, which tells of a merchant who was searching for fine pearls. On eventually finding one of great value, he went and sold everything that he had so that he could buy it (Matthew 13.45-6). The terse narrative is easily pictured in our imaginations. It implies that the merchant is engaged on a quest for precious, fine pearls. Perhaps he has already found some, accumulating a small collection. Delighted with the success of his search, he was about to return home. Then he came across another pearl, and everything changed. It was so beautiful and valuable that the others seemed dull and worthless. The outcome? He sold all the pearls he already had in order to possess and own the only one worth having. What he had once thought to be the best turned out merely to be good; and being good just wasn't good enough – only the best would do.

It is a telling illustration. All that the world has to offer pales into insignificance in the light of knowing God. This does not mean that our earthly loves, joys and hopes are to be seen as foolish things that we should condemn as evil. Good though they are, they are seen in a new light when confronted with the greater joy that is had through knowing God. This theme can be found at many points in the New Testament. Perhaps the most moving statement of the wonder of knowing God can be seen in Paul's letter to the Christians in the Roman colony of Philippi. After listing all his achievements, Paul comments on how they are all trivial compared with the unsurpassable richness of knowing Christ (Philippians 3.7-8): 'Whatever was to my profit, I now count as loss for the sake of Christ. What is more, I consider everything a loss compared to the surpassing greatness of knowing Christ Jesus my Lord.' These words resonate with the excitement of discovery and fulfilment. Paul had found something that ended his long quest for truth and meaning, just as the merchant found his special pearl.

One of the most powerful portrayals of the parable of the 'pearl of great price' is by the American artist Daniel Bonnell (born 1955). Commenting on his distinctive approach, Bonnell explained that his work almost invariably included 'two symbols'. The first of these in his painting *Pearl of Great Price* is the cross; the second is a single source of light that represents 'God the Father through the Son' to humanity. In this piece, Bonnell supplements the imagery of the merchant and his pearl with that of the parable immediately preceding it – the treasure hidden in a field (Matthew 13.44). The single source of light is provided by the setting sun, illuminating the scene from behind, as the merchant holds the precious pearl in his hands, captivated by its beauty.

To the right of the merchant stands a spade, which has been thrust into the ground after digging for treasure. Yet Bonnell uses it as the source of a cruciform shadow. The imagery of the cross now enters the illustration. Bonnell's point is simple: the precious pearl clasped in the merchant's hand is ultimately of such great price that no human wealth can purchase it, and no human achievement deserve it. It is given to us, as a gift, having been purchased by someone else. The ominous shadow of the cross reminds us of the costliness of this treasure, and our privilege in being offered it.

Yet there is a deeper issue here that resonates profoundly with the theme of this chapter. While very young, Bonnell recalls being forced to spend time alone in hospital. His family were not allowed to visit him for eight days. Though suffering the absence of his parents, Bonnell felt himself comforted by the presence of God. 'All my paintings, in an indirect way, lead back to those eight days left alone as a child. It is as if I had tasted being home in the broader heavenly sense of the word, while I was held by my heavenly Father. My life it seems is a journey to return home to Him once again.'

We see here a classic theme of Christian spirituality – the longing of the human soul to return to its creator. 'As a deer longs for flowing streams, so my soul longs for you, O God' (Psalm 42.1). God has created us with a homing instinct, with an inbuilt longing to return to our true home, even though this desire may be misdirected and misunderstood through weakness and sin.

It is a theme that is developed in one of George Herbert's most intriguing poems – *The Pulley*. In this poem, Herbert (1593–1633) explores the

idea that God, in creating humanity, foresaw a danger – namely, that we would adore God's gifts, rather than God himself. As a result, we might rest content with the good, failing to realize that the best lay beyond.

The poem speaks of God bestowing on humanity a variety of gifts and talents, such as strength, beauty, wisdom and pleasure. Yet God then 'made a stay'. God paused, and withheld one gift – the 'jewel' of rest. By creating humanity restless, Herbert argues, God hoped to prevent us from becoming satisfied with his material gifts. Humanity is perpetually dissatisfied, and this spiritual restlessness constantly throws us back to rediscover God. Using a mechanical analogy, Herbert suggests restlessness is like a pulley, which draws us towards God.

> When God at first made man,
> Having a glass of blessings standing by;
> Let us (said he) pour on him all we can:
> Let the world's riches, which dispersed lie,
> Contract into a span.

So strength first made a way;
Then beauty flow'd, then wisdom, honour, pleasure:
When almost all was out, God made a stay,
Perceiving that alone of all his treasure
Rest in the bottom lay.

For if I should (said he)
Bestow this jewel also on my creature,
He would adore my gifts instead of me,
And rest in Nature, not the God of Nature:
So both should losers be.

Yet let him keep the rest,
But keep them with repining restlessness:
Let him be rich and weary, that at least,
If goodness lead him not, yet weariness
May toss him to my breast.

Herbert's poem can be seen as a development of Augustine's prayer: 'You have made us for yourself, and our heart is restless until it finds its rest in you.' For Herbert, it is no accident that our heart is 'restless'. God has created it with this capacity, precisely in order to prevent us from becoming attached to the transitory things of life. Attachment to the world all too easily results in detachment from God. Rest is to be seen as God's final gift, bestowed upon us only when we finally enter his presence, and our hearts are at peace.

1 God as the heart's desire

Lord God, You have made us for yourself, and our hearts are restless until they rest in you. Grant us grace to desire you with our whole heart, that so desiring you, we may seek and find you, and so finding you, we may love you, and enjoy you for ever.

enfolded in the love of a personal God

_____

Christians believe in God. But what sort of God? The nineteenth-century poet Alfred Lord Tennyson slyly suggested that most Englishmen pictured God as an enormous clergyman with a long beard. Others have thought of God as a heavenly watchmaker who, having wound up the universe and set it going, left it to its own devices. It was against this type of idea of God that the French philosopher Blaise Pascal (1623–62) protested when he insisted Christians should speak about 'the God of Abraham, Isaac and Jacob, not of the philosophers'. More recently, the great physicist Albert Einstein (1879–1955) made it clear that, while he was no atheist, he did not believe in a personal God, but in the more philosophical notion of divinity found in the writings of Baruch Spinoza (1632–77): 'I believe in Spinoza's God who reveals himself in the orderly harmony of what exists, not in a God who concerns himself with fates and actions of human beings.'

When Christians talk about believing in God, they do not mean some vague generic idea of the divine, but about the specific God who called Abraham, Isaac and Jacob at the dawn of human history, and continues to call men and women today. Those great narratives tell of a God who speaks, who calls, and who makes promises – promises that are in turn trusted, and which lead to transformed lives (Genesis 12.1–4; 15. 1–6). It is impossible to make sense of them if God is thought of as an abstract, unknowable higher power. The God of Abraham, Isaac and Jacob is a personal God, who enters into a covenant relationship with individuals and therefore with his people.

This theme is developed in the Old Testament as the grand narrative of God's dealings with Israel unfolds. God leads his people out of Egypt and into the promised land. Throughout this great saga, God is portrayed as one who calls and loves Israel. This point is made with particular precision and clarity in one of the most theologically rich sections of the book of Deuteronomy:

It was not because you were more numerous than any other people that the LORD set his heart on you and chose you for you were the fewest of all peoples. It was because the LORD loved you and kept the oath that he swore to your ancestors, that the LORD has brought you out with a mighty hand, and redeemed you from the house of slavery, from the hand of Pharaoh king of Egypt (Deuteronomy 7. 7–8).

God is one who calls, leads – and loves. He is the one who remains faithful to those he calls, and enfolds his people in his love.

The visually rich idea of being enfolded in the love of God has understandably exercised a powerful grip on the Christian imagination. One of the finest explorations of this image is found in Julian of Norwich's *Revelations of Divine Love*. In this work, Julian (1342 – *c.* 1416) explains how her 'shewings' (a Middle English word now usually translated 'revelations') took place in May 1373. This tender extended meditation on God's eternal and all-embracing love is marked by its constant emphasis on the goodness of God and his love of the creation.

For many readers of the work, its most memorable and powerful feature is an image Julian uses to express God's commitment to his creation.

God is our clothing, who wraps and enfolds us for love, embraces us and shelters us, surrounds us with his love, which is so tender that he will never abandon us. And so in this vision I saw that he is everything which is good, as I understand it. And in this he showed me something small, no bigger than a hazelnut, lying in the palm of my hand, as it seemed to me, and it was as round as a ball. I looked at it with the eye of my understanding, and thought: What can this be? I was amazed that it could last, for I thought that because of its littleness it would

suddenly have perished into nothing. And I was answered in my
understanding: It lasts and always will last, because God loves it; and
thus everything has its being through the love of God.

Despite its weakness and frailty, the creation remains beloved by God, who
cares and provides for it. Despite all the trials and sorrows faced by God's
creatures, in the end 'all shall be well.' This note of reassurance is one of
the most distinctive and admired features of Julian's work. Yet this is not an
arbitrary aspiration, a baseless piece of optimism in the midst of despair.
It is grounded in the nature of God himself. All shall be well because God
constantly enfolds his creatures in his constant, upholding love.

There are many ways of exploring this point visually, and one of the
best of them is found in what is probably the best-known painting of the
Austrian symbolist artist Gustav Klimt (1862–1918), 'The Kiss' (1907–8). Klimt
famously presents a sumptuously garbed couple against a drab, uninteresting
background. The featureless, dreary world is transformed by love, of which
the kiss is a token. Klimt's couple are suspended in a moment of timelessness,
enfolded in a mutual love that shields them from the dull, ordinary world
around them. Their physical location and surroundings remain as they were;
yet at the deepest level, all has changed. They matter to one another; they
are significant; they are enfolded by each other's passion.

Klimt's portrayal of the transformative power of love, which can seem
at times to resemble a Byzantine icon, is a powerful stimulus to reflection
on the importance of love and relationships to human life. Love changes
everything, bringing value and meaning to individuals who might otherwise
feel unwanted, insignificant and marginalized. For Klimt, to be wrapped
up in love such as this is to be inside a precious and powerful cocoon,
which shields us from the grey grittiness of an impersonal, uncaring world.

Thus the dull background to Klimt's opulent depiction of a kiss is an ominous reminder that the existential transformation wrought through the recognition that we are loved may not greatly impact the world. But it is a starting point.

The gospel affirmation of the love of God for humanity penetrates to the heart of the human condition. It proclaims that we are 'clothed in righteousness divine' (Charles Wesley), enveloped by a love of a quality that it is ultimately beyond the power of human words to express. Klimt's brilliant, imaginative depiction of the alchemical potency of love to transmute the dull and mundane into the sumptuous and spiritual can be developed theologically to help us visualize the impact of the love of God on the believer. 'God is our clothing, who wraps and enfolds us' (Julian of Norwich).

This embracing, loving God is a personal God – a God who is able to enter into a relationship with individuals. The history of faith is replete with examples of men and women who discovered and experienced this transforming truth. We read of Abraham, who was called by God to go to an unknown country, and set in motion the great work of salvation. We read of Samuel, who heard the voice of God calling him in the night (1 Samuel 3.1–21). Or of John Wesley (1703–91), who found his heart 'strangely warmed', as he heard someone reading Martin Luther's account of the transforming power of God's grace. So how are we to understand this idea of a 'personal God'?

Although the specific term 'a personal God' is not found in the Bible, the basic ideas that come together to make up this important notion are all present. One of the most important of these is that God has a name, and tells us what this is. God is a 'You', not an 'It', to use language we shall explore later in this chapter. How many significant conversations begin with the question: 'What is your name?' For the writers of the Old Testament, naming something or someone implies that you have authority over them. For this reason, humans are not allowed to name God. Instead, God tells us who he is, and what he has done for us. In many ways, the Old Testament notion of the 'name of God' corresponds to what we would today understand by the 'person of God' – above all, the idea of faithfulness to promises.

One of the best attempts to clarify the idea of what we are to understand by the idea of a 'person' is found in the writings of the Austrian Jewish philosopher Martin Buber (1878–1965). Buber invites us to reflect on two different ways of encountering reality, which he terms 'I–It' and 'I–You'. In an 'I–It' encounter, the observer experiences something as impersonal – as an object. The English language draws an important distinction between 'knowing' and 'knowing about'. So think of a bag of sugar. We can know *about* a bag of sugar – for example, its weight, size or cost. But it makes little sense to say that we 'know' it. And still less to say that it 'knows' us.

The difference with an 'I–You' relationship is obvious and dramatic. There is far more to another person, someone who really matters to us, than their biological statistics such as their weight or the colour of their eyes. We *know* them, rather than just *know* about them. Buber's category of the 'I–You'

points to such a relationship being characterized by something much deeper – by a dialogical relationship, in which each party knows the other, and is committed to them. The relationship depends upon each party being willing to be known. Buber thus observed that an 'I–You' relationship depended on *grace* – on the willingness of both the 'I' and the 'You' to be known, with all the privilege and intimacy this implies. We know God (which is good) – but God knows us as well (which is even better).

This brings us to a central theme of the Christian understanding of God. *God wants us to know him.* Not just to know things about God, but to know God, and be known by God. God chose to enter into the human situation in order to make himself known and available to us. 'And the Word became flesh and lived among us, and we have seen his glory' (John 1.14). Spiritual growth thus has relatively little to do with accumulating knowledge about God; it is about deepening the quality of our relationship with him. Just as two friends might build their friendship by spending time with each other, so our relationship with God is nourished more by prayer and worship than by reading theology textbooks.

Thinking about a personal God also allows us to gain a deeper understanding of the nature of salvation. Consider the great Pauline statement that 'God was in Christ reconciling the world to himself' (2 Corinthians 5.19). The theme of 'reconciliation' concerns the restoration of a broken or damaged personal relationship between two people. Paul used the word in another context to refer to the reconciliation of an estranged husband and wife (1 Corinthians 7.11). The idea of being reconciled is fundamental to human experience, especially in the area of personal relationships. Perhaps the supreme illustration of its importance in the New Testament is the parable of the prodigal son (Luke 15.11–32). It illustrates vividly the reconciliation of father and son, and the restoration of their broken yet precious relationship.

This, then, is the God that Christians encounter in prayer and worship, in word and sacrament, and who enfolds and wraps us in his love. Words may fail us as we try to describe God's love; but God's love will never fail us as we try to bring its brilliance, richness and transformative power to the world around us. Christian thinking about this alluring love of God for humanity reaches a climax in the life and death of Jesus of Nazareth. As we saw in an earlier volume, Christians insist – with very good reason – that the only way of doing justice to the identity and actions of Jesus of Nazareth is to speak and think of him as God incarnate.

It is an idea that opens up some fascinating lines of thought. God became human so that we might become divine. God became small that we might become great. Yet perhaps the greatest of these thoughts is this: *God is Christlike*. Those three little words open up a way of thinking about God which forces us to recognize that abstract ideas of God are just not good enough to do justice to divine reality. Reflecting on Jesus of Nazareth brings us to a point at which we realize that a personal God has entered into history in personal form, calling individuals to faith and obedience, and demonstrating the love of God in his words and deeds.

Lord, help us to grasp how much we mean to you, and to bring that love to the world around us.

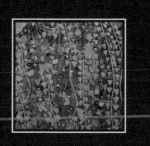

the lingering presence of evil

the lingering presence of evil

Every now and then, publishers produce sumptuously illustrated books about the Holy Land. These are often intended to help their readers get more out of reading the gospels. Their lavish photography informs our imaginations, allowing us to create mental images of the great gospel events. One of my favourite illustrations shows the sun setting over Lake Galilee. The scene is peaceful and irenic, the clouds tinged with the red hues of the sinking sun, complementing perfectly the famous lines of John Greenleaf Whittier (1807–92):

O, Sabbath rest of Galilee!
O, calm of hills above.

The scene is almost paradisiacal, echoing the calm and beauty of the created order that we associate with the Garden of Eden.

Yet nature's calm façade can turn violent with astonishing ease and unpredictability. In his painting The *Storm on the Sea of Galilee* (1633), Rembrandt depicts the violent storm that engulfed this same lake, terrifying Christ's disciples in their boat (Mark 4. 35–41). The placid freshwater sea that evoked a feeling of stillness and tranquillity was whipped up into a ferocious, seething cauldron, threatening destruction and loss of life. Rembrandt's dark, sombre tones express both the peril of the situation, and the fears of those caught up in the storm. The disciples are trapped by the titanic forces of nature, which they cannot hope to master. Where, they might well have wondered, was God in all of this?

It is a fair question. Yet it is one that can be answered from Rembrandt's superb depiction of the tempestuous event. For there, in the boat, is the one

whom the New Testament recognizes as the one who created all things, the word made flesh.

> A great windstorm arose, and the waves beat into the boat, so that the boat was already being swamped. But [Jesus] was in the stern, asleep on the cushion; and they woke him up and said to him, 'Teacher, do you not care that we are perishing?' He woke up and rebuked the wind, and said to the sea, 'Peace! Be still!' Then the wind ceased, and there was a dead calm. He said to them, 'Why are you afraid? Have you still no faith?' And they were filled with great awe and said to one another, 'Who then is this, that even the wind and the sea obey him?

At one level, this dramatic narrative can be interpreted as the creator asserting authority over creation, a theme we have already considered earlier in this series. Yet at another, it points to one of the most distinctive themes of the Christian understanding of God – the incarnation. God chose to be – and is – present in the midst of the turbulence, tension and tragedy of creation.

The imagery of water is enormously important here. The Old Testament makes it abundantly clear that the sea is part of God's original creation, part of the world of which God says that it is 'very good'. Yet it is from within precisely this 'good' creation that forces of chaos emerge, even if these are harnessed to bring about God's judgment. The sea is a potential source of chaos, of disorder, of destruction. It is viewed as a dark, fearsome, threatening place from which evil emerges, threatening God's people like a giant tidal wave and placing those who live near the coast in danger. Yet the flood that swamped the known world at the time of Noah is portrayed in terms of God unleashing the sea as a

cleansing force. At one and the same time, the sea eradicates sin and provides a medium of salvation for Noah and his ark.

The same pattern is found in the great narrative of the Exodus from Egypt. Moses and the people of Israel pass through the sea, which then engulfs their enemies. Once more, God uses the power of the natural world as a means both of destruction and of salvation. The sea, both as a physical reality and as a symbol of evil, is simultaneously part of God's good creation and part of the continuing source of chaos, destruction and terror. Yet God declares throughout Scripture that he is going to put the world to rights at the last, and wipe away every tear from every eye. This helps us understand one of the most intriguing features of the vision of the renewed and restored creation that we find in the book of Revelation. 'Then I saw a new heaven and a new earth; for the first heaven and the first earth had passed away, and the sea was no more' (Revelation 21.1). The sea, this dark and sinister force, seen as a threat to humanity, has been transformed into the River of Life. Like death, mourning, crying and pain, it has no place in the great renewal of things (Revelation 21. 4).

Yet humanity, as Augustine remarked, lives in the era between creation and consummation. We may indeed live in hope that one day, evil and suffering will be taken away. But how are we to live in the meantime? The great biblical narrative of redemption is framed by the memory of Eden and the hope of heaven; it is no accident that the first two chapters of the Bible are devoted to life in paradise, and its last two to life in heaven. Yet what we find in between these landmarks are ambiguity and tragedy. We live in the present with the past memory of Eden and future hope of the New Jerusalem.

Those who read the Bible hoping to find a neat solution to the intellectual conundrum of evil will come away disappointed, perhaps even frustrated. There are no easy answers. The Bible does not even appear to be particularly interested in the philosophical problem of how a good, all-powerful God could allow evil to exist; instead, it wants to talk about how God is dealing with the evil that we see around us. 'Evil is the force of anti-creation, anti-life, the force which opposes and seeks to deface and destroy God's good world of space, time and matter, and above all else God's image-bearing human creatures' (N. T. Wright). Instead of abstract philosophical analysis, we find a totally realistic affirmation of the reality of evil and suffering in history and in individuals' lives, and the utter determination of God to put things right – even though hindered by the madness and selfishness of humanity, supposedly the height of his creation.

This pattern is clear from the outset. As we read the deeply ambiguous story of Abraham and his descendants, the people whom God had called and chosen to help put things to right, we realize that humanity – even faithful humanity – is part of the problem. Time after time, we see the tragedy of the human condition playing itself out in the history of Israel. God redeemed Israel from captivity in Egypt. And what happened next? Israel comes close to reverting to paganism as it journeys through the wilderness on its way to the promised land. We find the same deeply ambiguous themes in the biblical accounts of Israel's entry into Canaan, during the period of the Judges, and then in the monarchy. David, the man after God's own heart, himself turns out to be deeply flawed – like everyone else. The kings of Israel lead the Israelites into great success at one point, and then into utter failure at the next.

It is not merely individuals that fail God, but institutions as well. Even the Temple itself, where God himself had lived in the midst of his people, was swept away as Babylon conquered and deported all who stood in its path. And yes, the people of Jerusalem were returned to their native Jerusalem with great joy after their exile was ended. But before long, the old problems re-emerged. The monsters began to emerge once more from the sea to threaten Israel. The history of Israel becomes dominated by the theme of oppression by the pagans – first the Greeks, and then the Romans. Israel again cried to their God to come and redeem her, to put the world to rights once and for all.

The New Testament shows how this great hope begins to be enacted through the life, death and resurrection of Jesus of Nazareth. To understand how God confronts evil, we must turn to the dark, brooding and troubling narratives of Gethsemane and Calvary. These speak to us of a God who chose to enter into the dark world of a fallen creation, and confront the monsters who emerged from the sea. As we read the gospel narratives, we see them all at work: human frailty, fallenness and faithlessness; the lure of wealth and power; the defection of institutions from their foundational purposes; the political power and corruption of the Herods and Pontius Pilates of

this world; the world of demonic, supernatural forces; injustice; betrayal; suffering. All are experienced and confronted by Jesus of Nazareth, as God incarnate. God thus takes responsibility for the creation, bearing the weight of its problems on his own shoulders.

Let us return to Rembrandt's vivid depiction of the storm-tossed boat containing Jesus and the disciples. It serves as a powerful symbol of the human situation. Many spiritual writers have likened the life of faith to a voyage through dangerous, uncharted waters to a safe harbour. We are at sea, at the mercy of forces over which we have no control. Yet Christ is present as we travel. God journeys with us, whether we pass through the valley of the shadow of death, or through the deep waters. Christ both affirms the presence and commitment of God as we travel through danger and uncertainty, and demonstrates and confirms that these dangers will one day be removed from us altogether. God is with his people as they cross the mighty waters, on their way to the New Jerusalem.

Life is precarious. The biblical writers knew that it was a precious gift from God, which was constantly under threat from natural forces and human agency. That was just the way things were. Today, we too often take the security of life for granted, failing to appreciate the insecurity of our existence. When tragedy happens, it devastates our blithe assumption that life is secure, and forces us to reconsider everything. Sometimes, it is through personal tragedy that we grow and mature in our faith. The growing interest in 'post-traumatic growth' is of major importance in this respect. An example will help make the point clearer. Appropriately enough, it concerns the sea.

In November 1873, Horatio G. Spafford, a Chicago lawyer whose family was deeply affected by the revivalist preaching of D. L. Moody, decided to travel to Europe. Business matters forced Spafford to delay his own departure. His wife and four daughters, however, set off on the *Ville du Havre* to sail to France. Spafford was to follow by the next available ship. The *Ville du Havre* collided with another ship, and sank. While Spafford's wife survived, his daughters all perished. Several months later, he travelled to the site of the sinking of the *Ville du Havre* and loss of his daughters. The experience moved him to write a hymn.

> When peace, like a river, attendeth my way,
> When sorrows like sea billows roll;
> Whatever my lot, Thou hast taught me to say,
> It is well, it is well with my soul.

Spafford made no attempt to resolve the intellectual difficulties attending the existence of evil in the world. For him, the existence of pain, sorrow and evil demanded something far more powerful than the resolution of some kind of intellectual puzzle. He wanted to be reassured that God was still there, in the midst of the chaos, pain and bewilderment of life. He needed to know that life still made sense and was worth living, despite these perplexing tragedies. As we contemplate Rembrandt's dark painting, we are reminded of something we must never be allowed to forget – that Christ, who is God incarnate, is in the same boat as the rest of us. He knows and understands what we have experienced – and what we fear. We may indeed walk through the valley of the shadow of death. But God is there, walking alongside us, our constant companion on life's long and winding road.

Lord, help us to cope with the bewilderment we so often experience as we contemplate the pain and sorrow of the world.

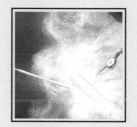

the Holy Spirit

the Holy Spirit

One of the most dramatic events described in the New Testament took place on the day of Pentecost. This Jewish feast, traditionally observed 50 days after the celebration of Passover, took on an entirely new meaning for the Christian community, in that it was the occasion of the coming of the Holy Spirit to the early church. This event, described in Acts 2.1–13, is understood to represent the fulfilment of the prophet Joel's vision of God pouring out his Spirit over all people, so that 'your sons and your daughters shall prophesy, your old men shall dream dreams, and your young men shall see visions' (Joel 2.28–32).

The coming of the Spirit is traditionally seen as marking the origins of the Christian church. The event is vividly depicted, in the realistic and dramatic style for which he became known, by the Milanese painter Pier Francesco Mazzucchelli (1573–1626), commonly known as 'il Morazzone' after the Lombardy village in which he was born. The painting shows the dramatic events taking place in the heavens, and their impact of bewilderment and amazement on those standing around. Intriguingly, Mazzucchelli depicts events from ground level, offering a highly unusual perspective on this familiar narrative. The observer is someone who has been thrown to the ground by this unexpected event, overwhelmed by its display of power and glory. The opening of the heavens is portrayed in dramatically realistic terms, with the 'fiery tongues' of the biblical account being represented by flashes of flame, originating from a dark heaven. The Holy Spirit is represented as a dove, surrounded by heavenly figures, echoing the revelation of God's glory at the calling of Isaiah (Isaiah 6.1–9).

So what is going on? We must never see this simply as a naked display of divine power, or an act of divine showmanship in which a flamboyant deity tries to impress an otherwise sceptical audience with an extensive special-effects department. There is far more to our understanding of the Holy Spirit

than a divine 'Look what I can do!' Rather, the coming of the Spirit is about God enabling his people to speak about the gospel with a wisdom, insight and energy that would otherwise lie beyond their bounds.

In beginning to think about the Holy Spirit, we need to remember that the Hebrew word *ruach*, used extensively in the Old Testament to refer to the Holy Spirit, has deeper associations and levels of meaning than most appreciate. To translate these nuances into English requires us to use at least three words – 'breath,' 'wind', and 'spirit'.

Perhaps the most obvious of these deeper levels of meaning is that the notion of the 'Spirit' is associated with life. According to the Old Testament creation account, God breathed into Adam, as a result of which he became a living being (Genesis 2.7). One of the clearest differences between a living and a dead human being is that the former breathes, and the latter does not. The Holy Spirit can thus be thought of as the divine breath of life. God is the one who breathes life into empty shells, and brings them to life. The famous vision of the valley of the dry bones (Ezekiel 37.1–14) makes this point beautifully. The collection of bones only fully comes to life when breath enters into them (Ezekiel 37.9–10). The New Testament takes this insight still further. God is not only the one who breathes life; he is the one who is able to restore that life in and through the resurrection.

The Old Testament often suggests a parallel between the power and activity of God and the wind. The Spirit is seen as God's creative shaping and moulding force, that great primeval wind blowing over the face of the waters, an image of the energy that God directs into his people and his purposes. The idea of 'power' is, of course, very abstract. It is all too easily dissociated from the people who exercise power, so that it is seen as an impersonal force rather than as a natural extension of the character and action of a personal being. Power is about the capacity to impose a being's character and will, often in

the face of obstacles. God is not power; rather, God is one who possesses the power to put into action what is demanded by his character.

It is an important point to appreciate. In a letter of 1887, John Emerich Edward Dalberg, Lord Acton (1834–1902), famously observed: 'Power tends to corrupt, and absolute power corrupts absolutely.' From this, he drew the conclusion that 'great men are almost always bad men'. It is an idea that has become part of the settled assumptions that govern our thinking about public office, and the risks of concentrating too much power in too few hands. Yet the Christian tradition has no place for any idea of a capricious, whimsical God, who takes delight in the unrestrained exercise of power. The biblical vision of God is one who chooses to limit himself; who is faithful to his promises; who cares for the widow and orphan; who chooses to experience the pain and suffering of humanity on the cross. Divine power concerns God's total commitment to the wellbeing of the creation, and whatever is necessary to bring about its renewal and restoration.

In thinking of the Holy Spirit as divine power, we must always contextualize this thought in terms of Jesus of Nazareth as the 'image of the invisible God' (Colossians 1.15). To talk about the 'almightiness' of God does not mean 'God's ability to do *anything*' but 'God's ability to achieve his good purposes'. God does not do things that deny his character, but always acts in accordance with who he is. And, as we emphasized in an earlier volume, who and what God is like are made known to us in Jesus of Nazareth.

Thinking of the Spirit of God in terms of the wind has long been an important theme in Christian spirituality. At times, God seems to be present in our lives or in history in a powerful and exciting way. At others, there are periods of calm, in which God does not give any indication of his presence. Like a sailing ship, we may find ourselves becalmed in the spiritual doldrums.

Yet this may suddenly give way to renewed divine activity, as the wind of God blows again in our lives and in history. The very unpredictability of the wind points to the fact that God acts in a way which we do not fully understand and cannot foresee. Spiritual writers such as Johann Geiler of Kaisersberg (1445–1510) compared the human soul with a sailing ship, stressing our need to ensure that our spiritual sails were ready to catch the breeze of the Spirit whenever it blew.

One aspect of God's activity that is illuminated by reflecting on the Spirit as wind is the complexity of God's dealings with humanity. Sometimes God acts, and is experienced, as a judge, one who breaks us down in order to humble us; at other times he acts, and is experienced, as one who refreshes us, just as water renews a dry land. Israel knew that a wind blowing in from the hot deserts to the east might wreak destruction and cause drought. For Old Testament writers, these scorching winds were an analogy for the way in which God demonstrated the finitude and transitoriness of his creation. 'The grass withers, the flower fades, when the breath of the Lord blows upon it' (Isaiah 40.7).

It was a reminder that God alone is permanent, whereas everything else is in a state of flux and change. 'The grass withers, the flower fades; but the word of our God will stand for ever' (Isaiah 40.8). The rise and fall of the earth's great empires is a powerful reminder of this point, so perfectly captured in the image of God as the scorching desert wind.

A change in the wind's direction, however, could lead to refreshment and renewal. The western winds blowing in from the sea brought rain and coolness to the land. Just as this wind brought refreshment, by moistening the dry ground in winter and cooling the heat of the day in summer, so God was understood to refresh human spiritual needs. In a series of powerful images, God is compared by the Old Testament writers with the rain brought by the western wind (Hosea 6.3), refreshing the land.

Yet there is an aspect of the Spirit's work that is not conveyed by the images of breath or wind. The *Spirit brings freedom*. 'Where the Spirit of the Lord is, there is freedom' (2 Corinthians 3.17) – freedom from the cultic rituals of the law, from the fear of death, and enslavement to the standards of the world. Freedom is a complex notion. We are liberated *from* things that enslave us. Thus the gospel liberates those who are 'held in slavery by the fear of death' (Hebrews 2.14–15). Yet we are also liberated *to* things and possibilities that we otherwise could never hope to achieve or possess – such as the hope of everlasting life. These ideas are often interlocked: for Christians, the gospel is about being set free *from* addiction to the possessions and values of this world, and being set free *to* enjoy the privilege of knowing Christ.

Many of these rich and varied themes are expressed in one of the Christian church's most famous hymns, *Veni Creator Spiritus* ('Come, Creator Spirit'), which is traditionally held to have been written by Rabanus Maurus (776–856). The poem was translated into English couplets by the great English poet John Dryden (1631–1700). Three of its stanzas are especially relevant to our theme in this chapter.

Creator Spirit, by whose aid
The world's foundations first were laid,
Come, visit ev'ry pious mind;
Come, pour thy joys on human kind;
From sin, and sorrow set us free;
And make thy temples worthy Thee.

Plenteous of grace, descend from high,
Rich in thy sev'n-fold energy!
Thou strength of his Almighty Hand,
Whose pow'r does heav'n and earth command:
Proceeding Spirit, our Defence,
Who do'st the gift of tongues dispence,
And crown'st thy gift with eloquence!

Refine and purge our earthly parts;
But, oh, inflame and fire our hearts!
Our frailties help, our vice control;
Submit the senses to the soul;
And when rebellious they are grown,
Then, lay thy hand, and hold 'em down.

Dryden's translation of this classic hymn to the spirit speaks of the 'energy' of the Spirit, and its capacity to inflame our hearts with love for God. At times, God encourages and exhorts; at others, he breaks and bends. God shapes and moulds us through his Spirit, sometimes breaking us down in order to build us up. Just as the surgeon may have to break a bone in order to reset it, so God must sometimes break before he can mend. Dryden's lines are a powerful reminder of God's role in encouraging and ensuring our spiritual development.

Yet the Holy Spirit is perhaps too easily thought of simply as the divine energy, channelled into the existence and lives of faithful yet needy human beings. The New Testament, while never losing sight of God's capacity and willingness to energize and enable his people, tends to focus the action of the Spirit on the person of Jesus of Nazareth. The fruit of the Spirit is fundamentally the creation of Christlikeness to bring about that great transformation of grace within us that leads to our becoming more like Jesus of Nazareth. As Paul points out, God has sent the Spirit of his Son into our hearts, crying 'Abba, Father.' The Spirit thus enables us to pray in a certain way – more precisely to pray as Jesus of Nazareth prayed, thus shaping us to be more like him.

This insight corrects a tendency that might otherwise emerge, in which we see the Spirit as the source and agent of impressive signs and wonders, designed to impress as much as to empower. The Spirit indeed empowers the powerless, and consoles the desolate. Yet perhaps most of all, he remakes us, helping us to crucify our old natures and bring to birth a new way of living and thinking – a way that the New Testament speaks of in terms of being 'conformed to Christ'. The Spirit leads us on to new depths of Christian discipleship, in which we come to be more like Jesus, the author and perfecter of our faith.

Lord, help us to love you properly. Set our hearts on fire with love for you.

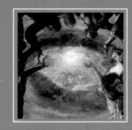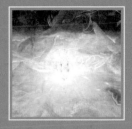

the mystery of God

the mystery of God

The language of theology sometimes seems to have little to do with the words we use in everyday life. For most people, the word 'hope', for example, means something like 'things we would very much like to be true (but suspect are not!)'. The deeper theological meaning of hope as 'a sure and confident expectation' seems to have been lost. We find the same problem with a word that occurs in Paul's exultant declaration that 'the mystery that has been hidden throughout the ages and generations but has now been revealed to his saints' (Colossians 1.26). Just what do we mean by this tantalizing word 'mystery'?

When I first began to study theology, the meaning of the word seemed obvious. A 'mystery' was a riddle, a conundrum, a brainteaser. I was an avid fan of detective fiction back in those days, and regularly pored over the stock in the second-hand book stalls in Oxford's covered market, searching for Erle Stanley Gardner novels to add to my collection. Colin Dexter's 'Inspector Morse' novels began to appear around this time, adding considerably to my delight, not least because they were set in Oxford. Perhaps inevitably, then, my theological understanding of 'mystery' came to be based largely on reading crime fiction! A mystery, as I saw it at that time, was a superficially baffling series of events, which could be explained by some sharp detective work.

So I read Paul's words in a similar way. The coming of Jesus Christ made sense of the complexities and obscurities of the Old Testament; its patterns of historical development, prophetic expectation, and divine involvement could only be rightly and properly interpreted through the life, birth and resurrection of Jesus of Nazareth. To use the language of crime fiction, the history of Israel was littered with clues to the meaning of life. C. S. Lewis

spoke of things in human experience – such as our moral sense – as 'clues to the meaning of the Universe'. The Christian faith, he argued, both made sense in itself, and made sense of what we observed in our own lives and in the world around us. As my interest in relating the natural sciences to Christian theology developed, I also began to explore the clues about the mystery of human existence that seemed to be embedded in the natural world. I saw no compelling reason to challenge my understanding of 'mystery'. It worked well enough. So why not leave it alone?

In the end, however, I began to realize that this understanding was inadequate, and did not really correspond to what the New Testament meant by the term 'mystery'. As I began to wrestle with writers such as Gregory of Nyssa, it became increasingly clear to me that there was another way of understanding the idea, which made a lot more sense of the New Testament. To speak of a 'mystery' is to recognize that the human mind cannot fully grasp the deep structures of reality. Christians realize that, in encountering the living God, we are confronted with something of such immensity that we cannot fully take it in, and have to content ourselves with incomplete and partial (yet reliable) accounts of what we experience. Both the New Testament and Christian spiritual writers use the term 'mystery' to refer to the hidden depths of the Christian faith which stretch beyond the reach of reason. To speak of God as a 'mystery' is not to lapse into some kind of obscurantism, or woolly ways of thinking; it is simply to admit the limits placed upon our human reason, and the hold it can obtain on the living God.

That is precisely the problem that we encounter as we try to take in the immensity of God. Without quite realizing what we are doing, we reduce God to what we can conceive, what we can cope with, rather than allow him to

challenge us to open our minds and hearts to his immensity, and enlarge our apprehension of his glory. We thus bring God down to our level, rather than allow him to raise us up to his.

The idea of mystery saturates one of the most famous narratives of the Old Testament: Moses and the burning bush (Exodus 3.1–9). While tending his flock in Horeb, Moses encounters the living God, and is overwhelmed by the experience. 'Moses hid his face, for he was afraid to look at God.' God meets Moses as he goes about his ordinary, everyday tasks; from that moment onwards, everything is different. The vision of God may have been too great for Moses to take in; yet it changed his life. Having declared that he was the 'God of your father, the God of Abraham, the God of Isaac, and the God of Jacob', God called Moses to liberate his people in his name. We see a similar pattern in the call of the prophet Isaiah (Isaiah 6. 1–9). Isaiah has a vision of the glory of God in the Temple, and is utterly overpowered by its immensity and grandeur. Yet this vision of God's glory is empowering, and leads Isaiah to offer himself for service. God's glory initially overwhelms us – but then energizes us.

William Blake (1757–1827) made this incident of the 'burning bush' the subject of a watercolour, which helps us to explore the incident in our imaginations. Interestingly, Blake appears to depict Moses as somewhat underwhelmed by his experience. He seems unmoved by what he observes; he gives little more than a sideways glance toward the 'burning bush'; and he makes no attempt to remove his sandals as a sign of reverence. Blake seems to be suggesting that Moses failed to realize the significance of what he observed, and challenges us to appreciate its mystery more fully.

In his *Varieties of Religious Experience* (1902), the famous Harvard psychologist William James (1842–1910) tried to draw together the characteristic features of human experiences that were attributed to an encounter with God. Perhaps most importantly, he noted that they were regularly described as 'ineffable'. An experience of this type 'defies expression', and cannot be described adequately in words. 'Its quality must be directly experienced; it cannot be imparted or transferred to others.' James also pointed out that such occurrences were found to be immensely significant by those who experienced them. They seemed to offer 'states of insight into depths of truth unplumbed by the discursive intellect'. He also noted their transience: they were often over before their full importance could be appreciated.

Now an experience may be ineffable; but that does not make it irrational or absurd. To develop James' point, we must insist that talking about the 'mystery of God' has nothing to do with irrationality. The Christian faith, as writers such as Thomas Aquinas remind us, does not contradict reason, but transcends it. Nor has it anything to do with the cultivation of obscurity or revelling in ambiguity and vagueness. It is a principled recognition of the limits of our capacity to cope with immensity. Augustine of Hippo's words may be noted here: 'If you can comprehend it, it's not God'. Our reason is unable to take in the vastness of the intellectual landscape of the divine, just as our words are unable fully to express what we encounter.

Augustine spent 20 years of his life writing *De Trinitate* ('On the Trinity'), a major treatise on the Christian understanding of God. A story – sadly, almost certainly apocryphal – is told about this book. Augustine was pacing up and down the Mediterranean shoreline close to the city of Hippo Regis, deep in thought. How, he wondered, could he hope to compress the immensity of God into words? While walking, he noticed a young boy filling a container with water drawn from the sea, and pouring it into a hole in the sand. Having done this, the boy did the same thing again and again.

Intrigued, Augustine asked the boy what he was doing. The boy replied that he was in the process of emptying the Mediterranean Sea into a hole he had dug in the sand. Augustine told the boy that he was wasting his time. He would never get the immensity of the ocean into such a small cavity in the sand. Unperturbed by this piece of well-intended criticism, the boy responded vigorously: 'And you're wasting your time writing a book about God. You'll never get God into a book.' The point made by the story is of immense importance to our theme. The human mind is simply not big enough to comprehend God in all his glory. God can no more be embraced and enfolded by our minds than the Mediterranean Sea can be squeezed into a tiny hole on a beach.

As the church reflected on the rich biblical witness to the words and deeds of God in Scripture, and her experience of God's presence in her life and worship, it became clear that the neat, simplistic philosophical slogans of the past were not going to be good enough to do justice to her majestic and glorious vision of God. A new way of thinking was needed. And so the

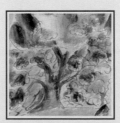

concept of the Trinity began to emerge – always slowly, initially tentatively, and finally conclusively. No better solution could be found, and subsequent theological reflection has yet to come up with anything better. In the end, we are forced to recognize that human words are simply inadequate to express the glory and wonder of God. When John Donne (1572–1631) spoke of the 'exceeding weight of glory', he was trying to articulate the intellectual difficulty of expressing the immensity of God. Similarly, Charles Gore (1853–1932) wrote of the Christian doctrine of God recognizing 'an awful sense of unfathomed depths beyond the little that is made known'. As recent studies of the psychology of human awe have emphasized, awe is the human response to something that exceeds our capacity to comprehend. Divine glory elicits our glad adoration, yet eludes our total comprehension.

So what pressures led to the emergence of this way of thinking and speaking about the mystery of God? Let's sketch some of its elements, focusing purely on the biblical material. Both the Old and the New Testament writers are emphatic that there is only one God, who is the God of Abraham,

Isaac and Jacob. 'Hear, O Israel: The Lord is our God, the Lord alone' (Deuteronomy 6.4). The four points in the Old Testament in which God speaks of himself in the plural (Genesis 1.26; 3.22; 11.7; Isaiah 6.8) are usually understood as 'plurals of majesty', or a 'royal we', although many Christian writers, such as Augustine, argued that these verses already contained hints of a Trinitarian way of thinking.

This theme is taken up, endorsed and echoed by the New Testament writers. At no point in the New Testament is any suggestion made that there is any God other than the one who created the world, led Israel to freedom and gave her the Law at Sinai. The God who liberated his people from their captivity in Egypt is the one and the same God who raised Jesus Christ from the dead.

The most significant factor leading to the emergence of Trinitarian ways of thinking is the basic Christian insight that Jesus is God incarnate – that in the face of Jesus Christ, we see none other than the living God himself. The New Testament even hints that he was active in the process of creation itself (John 1.3; Colossians 1.16; Hebrews 1.3). Jesus is the one who can be called God and Lord, who acts as creator, saviour and judge, who is worshipped, and to whom prayers are addressed.

Yet New Testament writers do not identify God with Jesus of Nazareth. Jesus refers to God as someone other than himself; he prays to God; and finally he commends his spirit to God as he dies. At no point does the New Testament even hint that the word 'God' ceases to refer to the one who is in heaven, and refers solely to Jesus Christ during the period of his earthly existence. It will now be obvious that we are beginning to wrestle with the real problem at issue. In one sense, Jesus is God; in another, he is not.

The situation is made still more complex, rather than resolved, through the New Testament's insistence that the Holy Spirit is somehow involved in our experience of both God and Jesus, without being identical to either of them (see, for example, John 16.14; 20.22; 1 John 4.2; 5.8). In some sense, Jesus Christ gives, or is the source of, the Spirit. Yet the Spirit and Jesus cannot be directly identified. The Spirit of God, which the Old Testament recognized as being present in the whole of creation, is now experienced and understood afresh as the Holy Spirit of the God and Father of our Lord Jesus Christ.

This brings us to the brink of what theologians often call 'the mystery of the Trinity', which we shall explore in the final two chapters of this book.

Lord, may we never rest content with simplifications and reductions about you, but long to know and see you as you really are.

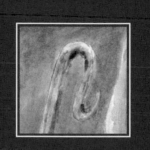   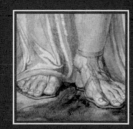

approaching the Trinity

approaching the Trinity

We all cherish childhood memories. I vividly recall going to church in rural Ireland as a young boy, on one of those relatively rare occasions when the entire Athanasian Creed was recited. In the wonderful language of the old Prayer Book, we declared our faith in 'the Father incomprehensible, the Son incomprehensible, and the Holy Ghost incomprehensible.' An old and slightly deaf farmer next to me gave the congregation the benefit of his considered judgment on these words. Speaking far more loudly than he realized, he remarked: 'The whole damn thing's incomprehensible'.

That, I fear, is how many Christians feel about the Trinity – something incomprehensible, combining mathematical absurdity with theological obscurantism. We can do without this sort of thing, can't we? Perhaps it is not surprising that most Christians rarely talk about the Trinity, even though they talk about God rather a lot.

One of the reasons why Christians find this so problematic is that the Trinity is difficult to visualize. St Patrick, the patron saint of my native Ireland, is believed to have used the leaf of a shamrock to illustrate how a single leaf could have three different elements. Gregory of Nyssa uses a series of analogies in his letters to help his readers grasp the reality of the Trinity, including the analogy of a chain. There are many links in a chain; yet to be connected to one is to be connected to all of them. In the same way, Gregory argues, someone who encounters the Holy Spirit also encounters the Father and the Son.

Christian art has always found it difficult to represent the Trinity. Many of the great medieval representations of the Trinity focus entirely on the Father and Son. We often have to search quite hard to find the Holy Spirit, who sometimes seems to be treated as little more than a theological afterthought. In his depiction of the Trinity, dating from 1491–4, Sandro Botticelli (1444–1510) uses the strongly devotional image of the crucifixion

of Christ as a means of anchoring the idea of the Trinity. Although there are many peripheral individuals in the painting – such as the angels, Mary Magdalene, John the Baptist, Tobias, and the archangel Raphael – the central figure of the painting is God the Father, who is portrayed as upholding his dying Son on the cross. It is a poignant rendering of the pain of God at the loss of his Son that shows Botticelli's artistic skills at their best.

Yet there is a theological point worth making here. The Spirit is represented in a curiously understated manner by a dove, hovering between the dominant figures of the Father and the crucified Son. While this is a deeply moving and powerful depiction of the love of the Father and the suffering of the Son, Botticelli seems to suggest that the Holy Spirit is less personal, less important, and somehow less connected with us than the two central figures of the great drama of salvation.

But why, many will wonder, do we need to talk about God in Trinitarian terms at all? Most of us probably feel that we know who and what God is without needing to think about the Trinity. God is the one who created this world and us. He is the 'God and Father of our Lord Jesus Christ' (1 Peter 1.3). He is the one who raised Jesus Christ from the dead. He is the one who knocks at the door of our life, gently asking to be admitted. He is the one whom we worship and adore, and to whom we pray, and so on. Yet the Christian understanding of God is *implicitly* Trinitarian. Theology simply makes *explicit* what is already *implicit* in Christian talk about God. Rigorous thinking about this God that we know, love and experience will eventually lead to the doctrine of the Trinity. Yet we don't really need to talk about Father, Son and Holy Spirit, in order to encounter or experience God. It is not the doctrine of the Trinity which underlies the Christian faith, but the living God whom we encounter through Jesus Christ in the power of the Holy Spirit – in other words, the God who is the Trinity.

Now there is no reason whatsoever why most Christians should want to become theologians, despite all the protests of those who (like myself) think that academic theology is a good, splendid and necessary thing. Most Christians want to keep their faith simple, and this wish must be respected. But underlying this apparently simple faith is a far from simple concept of God. When we begin to unpack the idea of God which underlies the New Testament witness and Christian experience, a remarkably complex idea, which strains the limits of human reason, begins to emerge.

To explore this point, let's explore a very simple view of God: the classical idea of God as the immortal, invisible, omnipotent and omniscient being who brought this world into existence but is not part of it. This sort of idea of God underlies much classical Greek and Roman thinking, and some modern ways of thinking about God (such as Deism and Unitarianism). It will be obvious that this view of God presents no real intellectual difficulties. It is easy to grasp, and involves no particularly difficult ideas, such as the divinity of Christ or the doctrine of the Trinity.

But what sort of God is this? The idea may be easy to understand, but can it bear the weight of the biblical witness and Christian experience? This is a God who is outside space and time, whom we have to discover, rather than a God who makes himself known. It is a God who is always beyond us, and not a God who comes to meet us where we are. It is a static, rather than a dynamic, God, who created in the past but cannot redeem in the present. And what of the future? What of the great themes of the Christian hope? In short, this view of God bears little resemblance to the God who makes himself known to us through Scripture, through the death and resurrection of Jesus Christ, and in Christian experience.

As a matter of historical fact, it was against this kind of view of God that the early church had to develop its doctrine of the Trinity, in order to prevent the 'God and Father of our Lord Jesus Christ' (1 Peter 1.3) becoming confused with this inadequate and deficient view of God. The Christian church was faced with a choice: it had to choose between a God who could be understood easily enough, but does not or could not redeem; or a God who redeems, and yet could not be easily understood. Rightly, as events proved, it adopted the second of these two options.

The 'classical theist' view of God is thus easy to understand, but fails to account for the biblical witness to and Christian experience of God. Christians know of God as a dynamic, pulsating activity, something or someone who is alive, rather than as some kind of static thing 'out there'. Simple faith knows of a God who is active, who makes himself known to us, who comes to us and meets us. Yet when we try to conceptualize this simple faith, we discover how complex and rich the Christian understanding of God actually is.

We could say that thinking of God as 'Father, Son and Holy Spirit' identifies the essential building-blocks that must be used if the full depth of the Christian experience and understanding of God is to be expressed adequately. No one picture, image or model of God is good enough. These three models are essential if the basic outline of the Christian understanding of God is to be preserved: the first model is that of the transcendent God who lies beyond the world, as its source and creator; the second is the 'human face of God', revealed in the person of Jesus Christ; the third is that of the immanent God who is present and active throughout his creation. The doctrine of the Trinity affirms that these three models combine to define the essential Christian insights into the God who raised Jesus Christ from the dead. None of them, taken on its own, is adequate to capture the richness of the Christian experience of God.

If God were only 'Father', we would have to think of him as the distant and far-removed creator of this world, who never becomes directly involved in its affairs. He would govern it from the safety of heaven, far removed from its problems and dangers, rather like a general directing his front-line troops from the safety of a far-off bomb-proof bunker. Yet this is not the view of God that we find in Scripture, nor in the long tradition of Christian experience of and reflection upon God. Again, if God were just 'Son', we would have to think of God being identical with Jesus Christ: Jesus is God, and God is Jesus. All of God would thus be concentrated in Jesus. Yet the New Testament is most careful to insist upon a distinction between Father and Son. God and Jesus cannot just be identified in this way. Again, if God were just 'Spirit', we would have to think of him as located within the natural world of nature, perhaps expressing this idea in terms similar to those used by nineteenth-century idealist philosophers. But, once more, Christians know that God just isn't like this. God is not reduced to being part of the natural process; he also stands over and against it.

And so we are forced to recognize the need to bring these three models or ways of visualizing God together, if an authentically Christian view of God is to result. Any one of them is only a starting point – the other two add perspective and depth. To talk of God as Father is really to talk about a one-dimensional God; to talk about God as Father and Son is really to talk about

a two-dimensional God; but to talk about God as Father, Son and Spirit is to talk about a three-dimensional God, God as we encounter him in the real world. Father, Son and the Holy Spirit are the essential building-blocks of the Christian understanding of God.

It would certainly be much simpler if God could be perfectly described using just one of these models, instead of all three. Yet we must deal with God as he is. Our intellectual systems will find themselves groaning under the strain of trying to accommodate God, like old wineskins trying to contain new wine.

One of the finest attempts to explain the doctrine of the Trinity to a lay audience is a small collection of 24 hymns by Charles Wesley (1707–88). For Wesley, hymns were not merely a means of praising God; they were an important instrument of theological education. So what should be more natural than to try to set out the basic themes of the doctrine of the Trinity in the form of a hymn? These short hymns manage to communicate and explain central Trinitarian ideas without technical language or theological fuss. This is one of the most effective of these hymns:

Father of Mankind be ever ador'd:
Thy Mercy we find, In sending our Lord,
To ransom and bless us; Thy Goodness we praise,
For sending in Jesus, Salvation by Grace.

O Son of His Love, Who deignest to die,
Our Curse to remove, Our Pardon to buy;
Accept our Thanksgiving, Almighty to save,
Who openest Heaven, To all that believe.

O Spirit of Love, Of Health, and of Power,
Thy working we prove; Thy Grace we adore,
Whose inward Revealing applies our Lord's Blood,
Attesting and sealing us Children of God.

The hymn sets out the idea of the 'economy of salvation' – the distinctively Christian understanding of the way in which salvation is effected in history. Wesley's concern is to identify its leading aspects, and show how the action of one and the same triune God can be seen in action throughout. Each person of the Trinity has its own distinctive role to play – a notion usually referred to as 'appropriation'. Every aspect of the great drama of redemption is shown to be interlocked. Father, Son and Spirit are woven into this great tapestry of divine salvation in a continuous narrative. Although Wesley's theology needs a little elaboration here and there, the fundamental purpose of the hymn is clear: to help congregations appreciate the manner in which the doctrine of the Trinity weaves together into a seamless garment the great threads of redemption.

6 | approaching the Trinity

So what difference does the doctrine of the Trinity make to the Christian life? Limits on space mean that we can only flag up a few points, each of which illustrates how this distinctively Christian way of thinking about God illuminates and informs our faith. We shall explore these in our final chapter.

Lord, help us to realize that we can never hope to grasp you in all your glory, wonder and majesty. May what we cannot grasp be the source of wonder and worship, rather than bewilderment and doubt.

the Trinity and the Christian life

'Our idea of God tells us more about ourselves than about Him' (Thomas Merton). Merton here reminds us that we are often tempted to construct ideas of God that resonate with our hopes, and which are adapted to our intellects. It is a point that features prominently in the writings of Karl Barth (1886–1968), now widely regarded as one of the greatest theologians of his age. Barth argued that humanity preferred to invent its own ideas of God and means of salvation. He saw the biblical image of the Tower of Babel as a powerful symbol of the human tendency to go its own way, and reach heaven on terms of its own choosing. Yet we need to be told, Barth insisted, what God is like. For Barth, one of Christian theology's most important tasks is therefore that of *iconoclasm* – breaking down our own cherished yet preconceived ideas about God, and replacing them with the real thing. It is no accident that Barth's approach led to the reinstatement of the doctrine of the Trinity as a cornerstone of Christian theology.

So why does this doctrine cause such difficulty for so many Christians? It is clear that many need reassurance that this doctrine is well grounded in the Bible, and that its apparent nonsensicality masks its capacity to be profoundly helpful in matters of faith. This small book can be seen as a small step in that direction – but one that needs extensive amplification in church study groups, Bible studies and college courses. Let me reiterate what the history of Christian theology has persistently shown to be the case: if the theologians of the church had not formulated the notion in its first centuries, their later successors would have had to invent it to make sense of the biblical witness and Christian experience.

Although we speak of the 'doctrine of the Trinity', what we really mean is the magnificent vision of God that transcends our capacity to understand, describe and explain what is tersely and inadequately summarized by this doctrine. When confronted with the mystery of God, the human mind

struggles to take in something that vastly exceeds its capacity to comprehend and to understand. It finds itself overwhelmed by the majesty of God, sometimes reduced to silence, at others to trying to put into words what it experiences, while knowing its words fail utterly to express what it has discovered to be true.

Without in any way underplaying the importance of doctrine, the Christian faith has always insisted that doctrines are secondary to the primary realities that they describe – in this case, the living and loving God, who is creator, redeemer and sustainer of all things. In his *Demonstration of the Apostolic Preaching*, Irenaeus of Lyons (*c.* 125 – *c.* 202), one of the church's earliest theologians to explore the Trinitarian dimensions of faith, affirmed his faith in:

> *God the Father uncreated*, who is uncontained, invisible, one God, creator of the universe; this is the first article of our faith. . . . And the *Word of God*, the Son of God, our Lord Jesus Christ, . . . who, in the fulness of time, in order to gather all things to himself, became a human being amongst human beings, capable of being seen and touched, to destroy death, bring life, and restore fellowship between God and humanity. And the *Holy Spirit*. . . who, in the fulness of time, was poured out in a new way on our human nature in order to renew humanity throughout the entire world in the sight of God.

On closer examination, this passage is not really concerned so much with the 'doctrine' of the Trinity in that narrow sense of the term, as with setting out a comprehensive account of all that God has done and achieved for his people. It weaves together the rich biblical material into a theological tapestry, shot through with themes of divine commitment, promise,

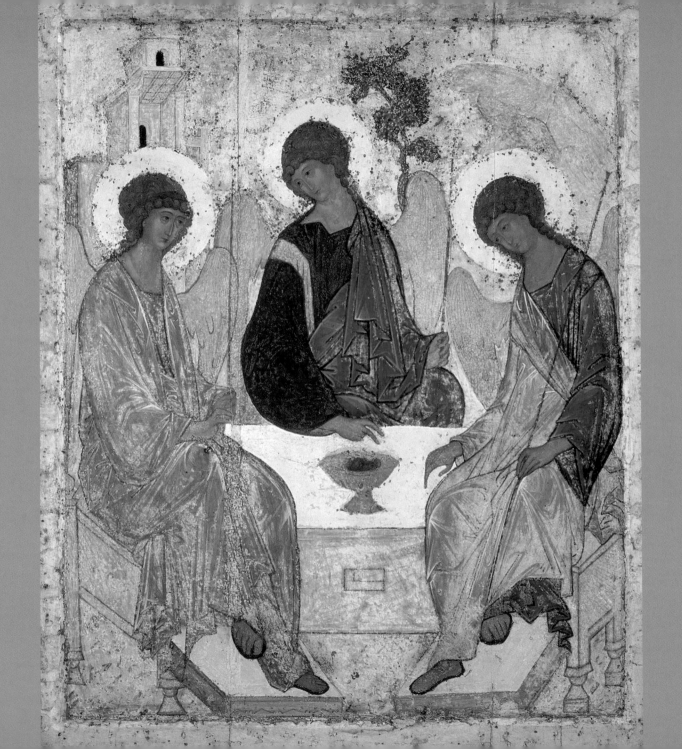

faithfulness and compassion. The doctrine of the Trinity does not introduce bizarre new ideas into the Christian faith, compromising its simplicity and making it appear unintelligible. Rather, it makes explicit the profound vision of God that underlies and undergirds our faith.

The doctrine of the Trinity thus gathers together the richness of the complex Christian understanding of God, to yield a vision of God to which the only appropriate response is adoration and devotion. The doctrine knits together into a coherent whole the Christian doctrines of creation, redemption and sanctification. By doing so, it sets before us a vision of a God who created the world, and whose glory can be seen reflected in the wonders of the natural order; a God who redeemed the world, whose love can be seen in the tender face of Christ; and a God who is present now in the lives of believers. In this sense, the doctrine can be said to 'preserve the mystery' of God, in the sense of ensuring that the Christian understanding of God is not impoverished through reductionism or rationalism.

The ancient hymn known as the 'Deer's cry' or 'St Patrick's Breastplate', traditionally ascribed to Patrick, patron saint of my native Ireland (c. 390 – c. 461), sets out a panoramic vision of God as creator, redeemer and sustainer, insisting that the believer is able to gain strength and encouragement by contemplating the majestic understanding of God which this doctrine unfolds. Although this hymn is known to many in the verse translation of Mrs Cecil Frances Alexander, we shall use some extracts from a more accurate version.

I arise through a mighty strength,
the invocation of the Trinity,
through belief in the Threeness,
through confession of the Oneness of the Creator of creation.

the Trinity and the Christian life

I arise today through the strength of Christ with his Baptism,
through the strength of his Crucifixion with his Burial
through the strength of his Resurrection with his Ascension,
through the strength of his descent for the Judgment of Doom.

I arise today, through the strength of Heaven:
light of Sun, brilliance of Moon, splendour of Fire,
speed of Lightning, swiftness of Wind, depth of Sea,
stability of Earth, firmness of Rock.

The hymn opens with a highly condensed statement of faith in the Trinity, expanded further in the lines that follow, which set out the landscape of faith that is illuminated by this doctrine. Patrick sees the Trinity as a recapitulation of the past actions of God, affirming both God's faithfulness and commitment to his people. Notice its emphasis on the awesome powers of nature, and the subtle inference that their power is subordinate to that of their creator. The titanic forces of nature are pointers to the still greater power of the one who created them. For Patrick, the concept of the Trinity fuses together the core elements of the biblical witness to God, causing us mental discomfort as we try to take it in, while at the same time moving us to worship as we appreciate just how glorious our God really is. For this reason, Thomas Aquinas (c. 1225–74), the great medieval theologian, suggested that theology was ultimately about being forced to one's knees in adoration of a mystery.

In this series of books, we have been exploring the importance of a *discipleship of the imagination*, in which we allow the great themes of the

Christian faith to control, nourish and delight us. In opening this series, I used an image, which may also serve to close it. I suggested that we are like people standing on the shore of a coral island, staring into the distance, seeing the ocean stretching ahead, with its gently undulating waves rippling. Yet beneath the surface lies an unseen world of coral outcrops, richly populated with marine plants and fishes, darting in the sun-dappled sea. The image reminds us that we often skim the surface of faith, failing to appreciate its hidden depths. Our thinking about God easily falls into this trap. The Trinity is an important corrective to simplistic accounts of our faith, inviting us to discover what lies beneath its surface.

So how can we visualize this rich vision of God? How can we move away from theological abstraction to the imaginative power of the visual? Patrick found the threefold structure of a shamrock leaf helpful in explaining the idea. Others would regard this as having severely limited usefulness in this matter, and would point instead to one of the most famous religious images: the icon of the Trinity, painted *c.* 1410 by the Russian artist Andrei Rublev (1360–1430). This icon is based on the Old Testament narrative of the three mysterious people who visited Abraham, as he camped by the oaks of Mamre (Genesis 18. 1–16). At one level, the icon can be seen simply as a representation of this meeting by an oak tree, at which Abraham offered his

guests the traditional hospitality of cooked lamb. Yet the icon clearly points to a deeper level of meaning and engagement. It is rightly regarded as a masterly rendering of some fundamental themes of Trinitarian theology and spirituality.

As we begin to explore the icon, we note that the Holy Spirit is to our right; the Son is in the middle; and the Father is seated to the left. Both the Spirit and Son gaze at the Father, who (according to Rublev's Orthodox theology) is the origin of both. Their heads are slightly bowed towards the Father, in acknowledgement of his ultimate authority. The Father's hand points towards the Son; the Son's towards the Spirit. It is a symbolic representation of the great pattern of revelation that we find in the New Testament, especially in John's gospel: the Father sends the Son; the Son sends the Spirit.

Each person of the Trinity is robed in a manner according to his distinctive role within the Godhead. The Father is dressed in a shimmering, iridescent robe, dominated by blue tones – a reminder that the Father, the king of heaven, is the ultimate source of all things. The Son is also robed in the same heavenly blue, supplemented with the dark red of clay – the fabric of the earth. The Son, Rublev reminds us, is the mediator between revelation and salvation, the one who bridges the gulf that separates the blue heavens and the red earth. In the incarnation, the creator has made himself a 'house of clay' (Thomas Pestel). On the Son's right shoulder, we notice a band of gold – an emblem of his authority.

The Spirit is clothed in blue and green, the colours of the natural world. We see here echoes of the Spirit's hovering over the deep, blue waters at creation (Genesis 1.1–3), and his continued presence in the living, green world. All of life on the earth – whether in its green pastures, the ocean's depths, or the skies – owes its existence to the divine breath of the Holy Spirit.

Yet our attention now shifts to the oak tree, just behind the Son. At first, we naturally regard this as one of the oaks of Mamre. On the table directly in front of the Son, we notice a dish containing lamb. At first, we naturally see this as an expression of Abraham's hospitality for his guests. Yet on further reflection, we realize that the tree is an allegory of the crucifixion, and the benefits that it brings. To use the rich imagery developed by Irenaeus of Lyons, the tree of death has, by the grace of God, become a tree of life. The lamb, in turn, points to Christ as the Lamb of God, who has taken away the sins of the world. We realize that Rublev is setting out a theology of the atonement, with strongly eucharistic overtones.

With that point in mind, we finally notice that the fourth side of the table remains open. There is room for another guest, who may eat of the fruit of the tree of life, and feast on the lamb of God. The perspective of the icon makes it clear that it is the viewer who is invited to occupy that empty seat. *The final place has been set for us.*

Rublev thus leaves us anticipating our own final encounter with the living and loving God, when we shall sit at table and feast with him and the saints in the New Jerusalem. The eucharist is a symbol, shadow and surety of this future great feast, reminding and reassuring us that we may live the

7 the Trinity and the Christian life

Christian life in its certain and glorious anticipation. This is a fitting point at which to bring this series to an end. We have celebrated the power of the Christian imagination, guided and nourished by the truths of the creeds, to visualize the truths of faith, and make us long to possess them fully. And one day we shall.

Lord, help us to long to see you as you really are, when we will feast in your presence in the New Jerusalem.

  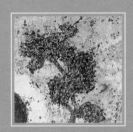 

further reading

Introductory

McGrath, Alister E., *Christian Theology: An Introduction*. 4th edn. Oxford:
    Blackwell, 2006, 203–71.
Vardy, Peter, *The Puzzle of God*. 3rd edn. London: Fount, 1999.
Wright, N. T., *Evil and the Justice of God*. London: SPCK, 2006.

More advanced

Adams, Marilyn McCord, *Horrendous Evils and the Goodness of God*. Ithaca, NY:
    Cornell University Press, 1999.
Ayres, Lewis, *Nicaea and its Legacy: An Approach to Fourth-Century Trinitarian
    Theology*. Oxford: Oxford University Press, 2005.
Davis, Stephen T., Daniel Kendall, and Gerald O'Collins, eds, *The Trinity: An
    Interdisciplinary Symposium on the Trinity*. Oxford: Oxford University
    Press, 2002.
Fretheim, Terence E., *The Suffering of God: An Old Testament Perspective*.
    Philadelphia: Fortress Press, 1984.
Grenz, Stanley M., *Rediscovering the Triune God: The Trinity in Contemporary
    Theology*. Minneapolis: Fortress Press, 2004.
Gunton, Colin E., *The Promise of Trinitarian Theology*. Edinburgh: Clark, 1991.
Hallman, Joseph M., *The Descent of God: Divine Suffering in History and Theology*.
    Minneapolis: Fortress Press, 1991.
Hart, David Bentley, *The Doors of the Sea: Where was God in the Tsunami?* Grand
    Rapids, Mich.: Eerdmans, 2005.
Hick, John, *Evil and the God of Love*. 2nd edn. London: Macmillan, 1977.
James, William, *The Varieties of Religious Experience*. London: Longmans, Green &
    Co., 1902.

Johnson, Elizabeth A., *She Who Is: The Mystery of God in Feminist Theological Discourse*. New York: Crossroad, 1992.

Kärkkäinen, Veli-Matti, *Trinity and Religious Pluralism: The Doctrine of the Trinity in Christian Theology of Religions*. Aldershot: Ashgate, 2004.

Keltner, Dacher, and Jonathan Haidt, 'Approaching Awe: A Moral, Spiritual and Aesthetic Emotion.' *Cognition and Emotion* 17 (2003): 297–314.

LaCugna, Catherine Mowry, *God for Us: The Trinity and Christian Life*. San Francisco: HarperSanFrancisco, 1993.

Langston, Scott M, *Exodus Through the Centuries*. Oxford: Blackwell, 2005.

Louth, Andrew, *Discerning the Mystery: An Essay on the Nature of Theology*. Oxford: Clarendon Press, 1983.

Moltmann, Jürgen, *The Trinity and the Kingdom of God: The Doctrine of God*. London: SCM Press, 1981.

Rahner, Karl, 'Remarks on the Dogmatic Treatise "De trinitate".' *Theological Investigations* (London: Darton, Longman and Todd, 1966), 77–102.

Torrance, Thomas F., *The Christian Doctrine of God: One Being, Three Persons*. Edinburgh: T. & T. Clark, 1996.

Volf, Miroslav, *After our Likeness: The Church as the Image of the Trinity*. Grand Rapids, Mich.: Eerdmans, 1998.

Wainwright, A. W., *The Trinity in the New Testament*. London: SPCK, 1969.

Wainwright, Geoffrey. 'Why Wesley Was a Trinitarian.' *The Drew Gateway 59* (Spring 1990): 26–43.

Weinandy, Thomas G., *The Father's Spirit of Sonship: Reconceiving the Trinity*. Edinburgh: T. & T. Clark, 1995.

Williams, Rowan, *Tokens of Trust: An Introduction to Christian Belief*. Norwich: Canterbury Press, 2007, 31–55.

Zurheide, Jeffry R., *When Faith is Tested: Pastoral Responses to Suffering and Tragic Death*. Minneapolis: Fortress Press, 1997.

illustrations

Pearl of Great Price by Daniel Bonnell (b. 1955), Private Collection, USA.

The Kiss, 1907–8 by Gustav Klimt (1862–1918), Österreichische Galerie Belvedere, Vienna, Austria, © 1990 Photo Scala, Florence.

The Storm on the Sea of Galilee, 1633 (oil on canvas) by Rembrandt Harmensz van Rijn (1606–1669, Dutch), Isabella Stewart Gardner Museum, Boston, USA / www.superstock. co.uk.

Pentecost by Pier Francesco Mazzucchelli, called Morazzone (1573–1626), Castello Sforzesco, Milan, Italy, © 1990 Photo Scala, Florence.

Moses and the Burning Bush by William Blake (1757–1827), © Victoria & Albert Museum, London, UK/ The Bridgeman Art Library.

The Holy Trinity with St John the Baptist, Mary Magdalene, Tobias and the Angel, c. 1490–95 (tempera on panel) by Sandro Botticelli (1444/5–1510), © Samuel Courtauld Trust, Courtauld Institute of Art Gallery, London, UK / The Bridgeman Art Library.

Icon with the Trinity by Andrei Rublev (1360– *c.* 1430), Tretyakov State Gallery, Moscow, Russia, © 1990 Photo Scala, Florence.